Know Yourself Choleric

by Alexander Carberry

COPYRIGHT
KNOW YOURSELF CHOLERIC

© Alexander Carberry 2022

First Edition published by:

Bahr Press

Cross Street Business Centre

43a Cross Street

Suite 10

Burton-upon-Trent

Staffordshire

DE14 3AR

United Kingdom

Written by: Alexander Carberry

Editor: Uthman Ibrahim-Morisson

Cover photograph: © Adobe Stock

Cover Design: Khadijah Carberry

A catalogue record of this book is available from the British Library.

ISBN-13: 978-0-9564513-3-0

About The Author

Alex Carberry was born in London England and was raised in Guyana South America on the edge of the Amazon. He returned to the United Kingdom to study but after meeting with a Sufi teacher chose instead to embark upon the Sufic path. He has spent 30 years studying Sufism, philosophy, geo-politics and Daoist martial arts. He is a practicing herbalist and resides in Burton-upon-Trent, England.

Contents

Dedication

In memory of all those that died in the COVID years of sorrow. Especially:

- Uncle Frank (Frankie) Armstrong
- Aunty Yvonne Armstrong
- Uncle Santon Carberry
- Shaykh Abdalqadir As-Sufi
- Hajj Naim Vancooten
- Hajjah Rahima Morrison

> They lived and loved deeply. With wide generous hearts, forgiveness and strength.

We belong to Allah and to Him
we return

The Noble Qur'an (2,156)

Introduction

Welcome! You have read 'Know Yourself: Discover Your True Nature with the Ancient Sufic Wisdom', and you now know that you're a Choleric. This book will provide a deeper insight into the experience of being Choleric.

By now, you will:

- also have gained useful insights into the personality types of those around you.

- and you have discovered the ability to accurately predict their various antics.

- The principle that, 'Apple trees produce apples and they do not produce Bananas!' is simply common sense, people are what they are. It is as if there is an inaudible music to which we are all dancing and now you are aware of another aspect of this universal, hidden music, as it sings its way through people.

If you are just reading this book out of interest and you are not a Choleric, I promise that the journey will be an interesting one. Cholerics may just be Cholerics, but there is an enormous amount of variation within this type. Though trees are just trees, there is immense variety and endless variations. People usually dislike the idea that they conform to a type, they find this limiting and simplistic, but on the contrary! Could you imagine being totally and constantly changeable? You would be utterly unable to master your own form. Your fixed form offers a consistent self-form to work with, providing a means to the possibility of self-mastery. Your type shows your natural energetic signature and we will see that no two Cholerics are the same, despite the striking similarities that characterise Cholerics as a whole. But a Choleric is a Choleric and that's just the way that they're wired.

A Choleric is a Choleric

Cholerics are in harmony with the Element of Fire. Fire reveals so much about you, it is powerful, hot, active, changes things, burns away excess and waste, it drives things forward, refines things and destroys. Brought into use with discipline and awareness of its power and danger, we can cook food, power cars, machines and jets but if we forget that discipline and awareness, it can destroy everything. Fire is pointed, focused and directional, it drives on and brings change. It separates and clarifies. Your energetic signature and purpose are very similar. The season you are in harmony with is summer, and you are like summer. Summer ripens the fruits of spring, brings forth brightly coloured flowers, it is hot, nurturing of activity and bringing things to fruition. In summer everything ripens and then will begin to dry out or the fruits will decay, and rapidly rot in severe heat. People socialise and enjoy themselves but those who know and are aware of the summer heat's destructive power tend to limit their activity in the sun.

Cholerics are like this, though they may vary, they are actively focused, bringing things to fruition, organising and marshalling, and driving activities to their ultimate goals. They communicate quickly, get to the point and love to take action. The underlying harmonies with the Element of Fire and the summer season are very instructive for Cholerics. As a Choleric these harmonies reveal the secrets of your purpose and your natural strengths and weaknesses. In this book we will really explore the Choleric and the various Choleric combinations. I promise you that you will discover more about yourself than you bargained for. Some things will be a comfort and a joy to know, whilst other things that you discover may be quite discomfiting; but Cholerics are not new to planet Earth and therefore, Cholerics have been facing the same challenges ever since mankind first appeared. Johann von Goethe said, 'If God had wanted me otherwise, He would have created me otherwise.'

You are a Choleric and that is just the way you are wired!

Apple Trees Do Not Produce Bananas

Apple trees do not produce bananas! Yes, it is obvious, and we all know that! But if you ask me whether you can change your type, you are suggesting that apple trees might produce bananas. You are you and that's that, get over it! If you accept that an apple tree will never produce bananas or vice versa, then we are better off working with the natures that we already have, rather than wasting time wishing that we had been different. The fixed self-form we possess gives us an identifiable starting point to work from, as opposed to being an unyielding cast iron cage. We may mould, change and transform ourselves but we are working with the same basic pattern material. The energetic signature that we start with will continue to be expressed in endless ways. We will always recognise a Wagnerian Opera when we hear one, or a Beethoven or Brahms symphony. We will always recognise Jimi Hendrix, Amy Winehouse or Deep Purple. There is a very clear signature to them all. With all of us it sings through our DNA, our voices and the sound of our footsteps. It characterises us. We smell of it, we are it, and those that love us love it, and those that hate us hate it. We are certainly not here to please everyone (and what a thankless task that would be!). This is our song and no one else's. This is just the way that we are. We can change countless things about ourselves. Changing, developing and strengthening all bring growth, but our energetic signature will always remain the same. As Erasmus of Rotterdam said, "It is the chiefest point of happiness that a man is willing to be what he is." Wise words! Wise words indeed.

You are what you are, and your personality type is a description of the energetic signature of your psyche, which is from the Greek for breath, its Sufic equivalent is the Arabic word ruh (pronounced roo - h), which also means breath. Both the Greek word psyche and the Arabic word ruh refer to the soul. What we are examining is the very patterning of souls. Apple trees do not produce bananas and that is just the way it is.

The Forest and the Trees

A personality type is like a forest of pine fir trees, though all the pine trees are similar and from the same family of trees. Every one of them is unique. Amongst them are groups of trees that possess similar traits. In this book I will show you the various types of Cholerics and how they differ.

What You Will Get from This Book

Since this book is about Cholerics, expect it to deliver just that. If you want the details of the other types then read:

• Know Yourself Sanguine;

• Know Yourself Melancholic;

• And Know Yourself Phlegmatic.

What we will develop in this book is the ability to look at ourselves in the manner that an artist may look at a painting. With attention to the details, seeing the brushstrokes, the hues, tones and richness of colour. We will look at proportions, the composition and the perspective. Then you will be able to say this is a Dali, a Kahlo or a Matisse. You will develop the art of seeing the texture of your own personality, and this is the same skill that you will utilise to examine others. This skill will be yours forever and you will be able to rely on it to understand your greatest and only true wealth, which is your own self. By getting to know yourself, you will efficiently learn to know others.

You will gain tips on dealing with aspects of your personality that you may find difficult and will also explore how to turn them to your advantage. You will get an insight into your own genius - that is genius used in the original Latin sense of 'your natural inclination or natural abilities'. You have a genius and there is not another genius quite like yours on the entire planet. Playing to your genius and avoiding the areas in which you are naturally weak will give you a strategic advantage. You will learn that once you engage in an area in which you are naturally weak, then you have to have a plan and utilise some techniques to avoid or get out of trouble. For those who are not Cholerics, you will get tips on how to deal with difficult Cholerics. I want you to be the best you can be, and so I will share everything that I believe will help you to achieve that. This series is designed to be short and easy to read, you should be able to read one of these books quickly and smoothly. So, within these limits, I will share as much as I can.

Let Others Be What They Are

If you are not convinced that people are just the way they are because they are wired that way, then I suspect that by the end of this book it will become much more difficult for you to hold onto the idea that human beings are like plastic and so can be moulded in any way that we like. Calling it evolution, or whatsoever else you choose to call the desire to make something what it is not, will not change the truth of what people are. We are simply what we are. When we accept this and get on with the job of dealing with ourselves, then we give ourselves permission to allow others to be as they are. We do not have to make them into clones of ourselves or someone else. We have to let ourselves and others be who and what we all are. We can strengthen natural strengths, find strategies to deal with natural weaknesses, and thank God, we can tell each other off for the bad habits. But remember, we are what we are, and if you are determined to make a lion out of an elephant, then good luck with that. If you fancy a bet, I'll tell you for free that the odds are heavily stacked against you succeeding! What is worse, it is a tyranny that we inflict upon ourselves and upon others, to try to force ourselves and each other to be what we are not, it simply won't work. As everyday life continues to demonstrate.

How To Read This Book

Go through the contents page and take a quick look at anything that arouses your attention. This will stimulate your interest, provide you with an overview of the book's structure, as well as encourage you to read it. It may also be helpful to read the book once quickly, from cover to cover. Things are much easier to remember and make use of if you remember their context. After reading through once, then return to the parts that you feel you need to re-read and reflect upon.

Discuss some of the ideas and concepts with those around you. One of the easiest ways to learn and remember is to share what you know. Question those who have known you for a long time about the way they see you. Observe carefully the way you and others do things. Remember, you do not have to like something for it to be true. Certain home truths can taste very bitter at first, but the surprise sweetener lies in accepting things for what they are and avoiding the truly bitter lesson of time and energy painfully and uselessly wasted beating one's head against a brick wall; things are what they are!. You will discover much about yourself that you like and much that you do not like. What we are working towards is not liking what we see but surrendering to the truth or reality of things as they are. However much we may dislike it, redness will not be transformed! We may change the shade, tone and hue of the colour red, but redness will always remain a permanent feature. Our fundamental nature is analogous to colouring in this respect. Read the book, make your observations and once they become truly clear to you, accept them. Acceptance is not such a difficult step. Remember the stories that we tell ourselves about ourselves and everything else, are just stories; the way things really are transcends our stories. Over time our dislike and resistance to the way things are, will change to acceptance. At that point we are free to work with what is there, rather than attempting to maintain an illusion. Over time and with practice our need to persist with our favourite stories in the face of reality diminishes.

Welcome to the Journey

Congratulations you have made it this far. Let us continue our journey into the depths of our personality type, to encounter the treasures, the lovely surprises and all the wonders that are waiting to be discovered. I continue to be fascinated by this knowledge and am really excited about sharing it with you. I hope that you will be even more fascinated than I have been, and I pray that you will continue to find it more and more useful, as you continue to work with your true self.

The amazing thing about the Universe is that just the act of discovering something new and transformational, means that the entire Universe has, in fact, changed. Everything is changing and yet it all remains the same! Transformation is the very nature of the Universe, and you are not separate from it. You were born to be what you are and to be the best that you can be.

Will the reward of doing good be anything

Other than good?

So which of the favours of your Lord do

You both deny?
The Noble Qur'an: 55:60-61

A Picture of the Choleric

She was a force of nature. In action (and she was always doing something), she drove ahead and did not suffer others getting in her way. Her determined gait let all know that she was not to be trifled with, her firm but femininely militant stance commanded her ground and her bright eyes held purpose in them. She never laughed at a joke that she did not find funny, resisted others' invasion of her space and became easily bored with a conversation in which she perceived no point. Her intellect was like quicksilver, rapid, sure, intuitive and incisive. Her tongue sharp, cutting and strong. She held things together and could be depended upon. Yes! She is one of us! She is a Choleric!

Description of the Choleric

Cholerics possess purpose, strong intent and willpower. They are made for action and are aggressive in that. Their considerable social intelligence is focused upon marshalling people and situations. They know intuitively, quickly and surely. This swift natural intelligence cuts to the core of things and they are usually right. They get swiftly to the point and have a very low patience threshold for waffle. Cholerics enjoy it when there is action, which leaves them free to act and manoeuvre; deny them this and they become frustrated and explosive. Their impulse is to drive forward, to change things to develop them and they are resistant to being given orders. Herein lies the difficulty, Cholerics like giving orders and hate receiving them and this provides them with the challenge that can be their Achilles heel, as a result they can inspire extreme resentment from those who have worked this out, and that is always counterproductive and corrosive when working within a team. This focused form changes often but can lack flexibility once they are committed, there can be surprisingly little flexibility when this happens. Paradoxically, this can suddenly change if they realise that there is no future in the current course of action. They then change with a rapidity and ruthlessness that can leave other types reeling. They will not suffer being boxed in, though they will rapidly close their own options down in order to commit to and complete their current project. Expect them to be passionate, loyal and prickly. Do not get in their way, obstruct or restrict them unless you are looking for a fight and if you go there, you will certainly get one!

The Choleric in Action

John is the manager, he is either very well dressed or has thrown everything on, whatever else happens, there will be some dash of bright colour. Reds, yellows and oranges being particularly popular. He moves swiftly and purposefully, greeting quickly or not at all, and seems eager to get started. If people appear to be 'idling' he will let them have it. Generally, he cares less about them liking him than getting the job done. He draws attention to himself by his command of his personal zone and doesn't like people getting into his 'personal space' though he will often invade yours. He remembers people's abilities and less so their names. He engages swiftly in conversation if there is something to deal with and will swiftly disengage once the purpose of the engagement is completed. Swiftness, manoeuvrability and focus characterise him. Sitting doing nothing becomes interminable for John, making him red-faced, frustrated and troublesome.

John will often say things that seem incredibly insensitive as he drives straight to the point. If, however, he sets out to master social skills he will work at it with gusto, with a directness and determination that is unique amongst these types, though you will always see that John does not suffer fools gladly. He does not like to fail. Fear of failure will drive him to work and some of his species must have mastery of what they are involved in or they will not engage at all. He loves to win and expects to do so.

This is the description of a very strong Choleric, in whom we see very little evidence of the other elements or personality types. Some of this, if not all of it, will probably ring true for you.

The World According to the Choleric

Let us imagine a Choleric describing themselves. It is probably a CV or an interview:

Interviewer: "How would you describe yourself?"

Choleric: "I am a go getter, very focussed and to the point. I love to do things that make a difference. I would describe myself as hardworking."

Interviewer: "That's interesting, because looking at your profile you have done a considerable amount. Would it be accurate to describe you as a serial achiever?"

Choleric: "Yes, that would be accurate. Whilst many people may procrastinate, I like to get the job done quickly and move on to something else. Yes! I can't remember anyone calling me that before, but yes! Serial achiever is an accurate description of me."

Interviewer: "Would you describe yourself as friendly, perhaps a people person?"

Choleric: "Hhhmmm! I have been thinking about this one. I was on holiday in Bali, the weather changed and I was stuck in a cottage with my travel companions for three days. There was nothing to do, or so it appeared for the first three hours, I almost died of boredom and my friends began to really irritate me with their pointless conversations and lazing around. Eventually, I could take it no longer and exploded, then I caught myself and approached the problem from another angle. I organised three days of games and activities and invited the guests from some of the other cottages to take part. I enjoy peoples' company, but we have to be doing something, there must be a point to it!"

Interviewer: "What would you describe as your greatest strength?"

Choleric: "Isn't that obvious? I am an organiser, I get things done and keep people busy! When I'm around things are achieved."

Things I Hate

Interviewer: "What are the things you hate?"

Choleric: "Doing nothing! Pointless conversations! Laziness! People who don't get to the point; Endless waffle is unbearable! Stupidity! Procrastination! Things that take a long time to do, especially when it can be done faster and better! People who won't move on; Yes, there was a problem! Now fix it and move on. What is the use of dwelling in the past? I also hate losing. I can't stand losing at all!"

Interviewer: "Anything you hate about yourself?"

Choleric: "Not being able to relax. I need to keep moving and doing. Sometimes I'm a little envious of people who find it easy to relax, but it would be unbearable to sit there doing nothing. So, I find ways of relaxing actively, like swimming and boxing."

Interviewer: "Boxing!"

Choleric: laughs, "You wouldn't understand! It gets a lot out of me and at the end I am tired and experience a kind of tranquillity, my body really relaxes after having a good go at the punching bag."

Interviewer: "Do you hate awkward situations?"

Choleric: "That really isn't my problem. I fix things and then move on. If it can't be fixed, then you shouldn't waste time. If it can't be fixed it's time to move on."

My Outlook

Interviewer: "What is your outlook on life? What motivates you?"

Choleric: "Haven't I answered that question already?"

Interviewer: "No, I haven't asked it before!"

Choleric: a little irritated, "You've asked a number of questions and from my answers my attitude to life should really be clear by now. Life is short and there is loads to do, so we should keep ourselves busy doing the things that need to be done. Your interview is supposed to take 15 minutes and 15 minutes is now up. It has been a pleasure chatting with you but now I must go because I have to be back at the office by 10:30."

The Choleric According to the Rest Of The World

The Good Points

It is extremely useful to be able to see yourself through others' eyes. It can make all the difference. Cholerics are really valued for their natural organisational skills, swift and intuitive grasp of situations and their tendency to look after people close to them. This can actually make them lovable. Though Cholerics can sometimes be easily offended, they tend to move on quickly. They are generally thick skinned and will come up with ripostes at lightning speed. They are not generally dramatic and get to the point quickly. People can feel safe around balanced Cholerics because they are loyal and protect those close to them. When a Choleric is for you, they are for you, but don't you dare cross them!

The Complaints

Cholerics can be overbearing, controlling, so convinced of their correctness that they never listen and can be aggressive to the point of belligerence. You really don't want a Choleric as an enemy. They have a no prisoners approach and push towards the goal, accepting consequences that the other types will recoil at. This often alienates people who work with them.

Cholerics will shoot your idea down, with criticisms, only for you to see your idea reappear as their own two weeks later! They don't remember who they got it from and will narrate it to you with the certainty that you've never heard it before, and as indisputable wisdom. Reminding them of its origin only gains you an irritated response. When they feel strongly about something they can be very hard to work with, especially if a differing perspective is required and you are the person providing it. It can, however, be fun to sit back and watch the fireworks as arguments ensue when the Choleric and the other person fight it out (and the Choleric has to win). It is such a predictable scenario with an undeveloped imbalanced Choleric, that it is a sure thing. Seasoned gamblers would refuse to take odds on this one!

Though Cholerics can be belligerent, confident and combative, they will at times melt down, revealing a tender, sensitive centre that can be very deeply hurt and it takes a long time for the other types to figure this out and learn to work with it. The more this deep sensitivity is hurt, the more combative, unstable and irrational a

Choleric becomes. An out of balance Choleric can be impossible to live with! To pick up the pieces and help you work through these phases we need to don some armour and prepare ourselves for your lashing out, flailing and rage. This is a job for the truly courageous. You will say things that wound deeply and that hurt; it is as if your only intent at that time is to share your pain. For those of you Cholerics who keep going, getting to some healing beyond this, then you move on quickly (your thanks and remorse don't last very long).

If you Cholerics take us on as one of your projects, you are usually convinced that you are more correct about our situations than we are. You are often correct, but it is a tiresome and infuriating experience, and we will often be left wondering whether the results were worth the experience. We just wish you would learn to listen more.

You won't let us finish what we have to say. You interrupt, finish our sentences and take things in directions you feel are not pointless. Some of us take a long time to say what we have to say and an even longer time to work out what we want to say. When you interrupt us, it takes a long time for us to regather our thoughts and to be able to find the will to express them. This, of course, convinces you that you were right, because we had nothing to say in the first place. You could not be more wrong. At close quarters this is impossible to deal with every day, and so often we walk away for the sake of self-preservation. You don't do affection much, and if it gets in the way of what you want to do, it is so obvious that it is an absolute turn off.

We accuse you of something you didn't do, and you will not give an inch until it is corrected. You accuse us of something we didn't do, and like you, we choose to stand our ground, you simply look at us as if we were stupid for wasting so much time and effort on so trifling a thing.

Now, I can easily continue! The point is that every one of your strengths used inappropriately, will tend to become a weakness. Wisdom is knowing what to do in its right time. The wise read the situation, are aware of the differing perspectives, perceive the directions in which the situation is headed and draw upon their natural skills to help the situation to move on to the next stage. If we act blindly then we invariably act inappropriately. Wisdom, not ideals and principles, leads situations to balanced healthy outcomes. Default behaviour, ideals and principles lead us blindly into outcomes that do not consider health and balance. Wisdom allows us to observe what is happening, to draw upon our knowledge and experience and to respond appropriately. This is what responsibility truly is.

To achieve balance, whatsoever our type, the default behaviour of our natural form must be addressed so that we can respond with awareness and responsibility. Without this our responses are blind and lack responsibility. There is so much that you can do and bring about, but to do this you must learn to get the best out of your given form.

You Cholerics are a force of nature. Like summer and fire, you bring movement, ripening and change. To master your harmony with your energetic impulse and purpose will take a lifetime of constant work. Now, there's a challenge for a Choleric if ever there was one!

Spot The Choleric

"You can tell a Choleric by their openly direct and single-minded attitude. They arrive quickly at decisions. Their thought is quick and instinctive; they just know.

They arrive at quick judgements and are usually right. As a result of this they tend to have very little time for those who disagree with them. For a pure Choleric, if you do not agree with them, you can't be all that smart. They lead from the front, don't take any prisoners and drive ahead relentlessly."

Spot the Choleric - From Know Yourself: Discover Your True Nature with the Ancient Sufic Wisdom

So Why Are You Like This?

You are like fire and summer. What characterises summer characterises you: heat, activity, fun, focus, energy, ripening and ripened fruits, the urgency to reap the fruits, flowering, bright colours, moving swiftly on, making use of all the wonderful summer days, ripening and maturity. Summer is the pinnacle and once the pinnacle is reached the fruits, flowers and green growth decays. Cholerics are aware of this reality on an intuitive level. Their actions are always in harmony with this reality. Their movements are swift, choppy and they seem to march in an almost military fashion. The Choleric woman in high heels marches out purposefully, stepping with a very sharp click on every step. Her colours will be bright, reds, oranges and yellows tend to feature. The men march forward chest out, expressing the same energy in a very similar way. You will speak and gesticulate with chopping movements of the hand to accentuate points and you may even point, with firm resolution. You stand with feet set a shoulder's width apart, weight sunk down, firmly rooted and ready to move ahead. You unconsciously close down the space between you and others, but cannot stand it when it's being done to you. You also sit in this manner. This is the music resounding through you, striking the gong of your being and keeping it singing in that uniquely Choleric way. But you will have to learn to understand how that music may be heard by other types. The 'wetter' types will find that you restrict them and may kick against it, and the 'colder' more introverted types will find you loud, shocking and a little bombastic, sometimes with them even your gentleness may be a little overwhelming.

Your focus, foresight and drive towards a goal are great gifts to humanity, very much as summer is. You must learn to use this inner music and Choleric rhythm to marshal things on in a smooth uncomplicated way with as little conflict as possible. This is your genius, and you must learn to use it well. Gaining insights into the mastery of its secrets will take a lifetime of active study. Being Choleric is a great adventure, so understand when outward movement is required and when inward mastery is the goal. For without the mastery of yourself you will be imbalanced and unnecessarily combative. Sometimes the combative is the way to get things done but its overuse will render it ineffective in the long run.

Since you are like fire it is instructive to reflect upon the undisciplined raging and destructive power of a forest fire. Get onto youtube if you haven't seen or experienced one and look at news reports or documentaries about bush fires. I have experienced them, and they are raging destructive forces of nature that destroy everything in their path indiscriminately. Reflect also upon the fire with which you cook your food. This is a controlled disciplined power, which is able to deliver the right amount of heat to bring about a very specific result. Engines are usually powered by fire and we see the not so gentle but controlled disciplined power expressed in jet engines. I remember receiving a few cauterisations as a child, and this disciplined application of fire has more than once saved my life. Fire is in harmony with you and will bring renewal, staring into an open fire will be one of the few times that you can sit still and be utterly absorbed. This is one activity which will relax, still and rejuvenate you.

Remember, fire needs fuel and so if your activity outstrips your energetic reserves then it doesn't require a genius to work out what will happen.

Choleric Relationships

In relationships you act, do and give, by making things happen. You show your appreciation by giving, supporting and helping but on your terms. You are not particularly affectionate, frequent touching and prolonged closeness is just not you. You need to stand apart, have space and not feel smothered, and you do not react well to being smothered. You will tend to give, serve and do things that support, without much emotional display and expect people to know that you did so because you care about them. Too many emotional displays tend to make you uncomfortable. Emotional displays and closeness that gets in the way of what you want to do, is particularly irritating. Flames drive up and onward and burn what is in their way, and like fire, you will become quite prickly when people approach you with hugs, kisses and puppy playfulness when you are focused upon something else. Once you are focused this does not change easily and since you feel pressure to complete things and close your options down, anything that gets in the way is experienced as deeply uncomfortable and irritating. Since you also look to see what is needed and then execute it, remember that others may not have perceived what you have, and you may find your support unwelcome.

The Choleric tendency to communicate by getting straight to the point, often abruptly and with certainty will often be misinterpreted in relationships. Other types just deal with these things in very different ways and often context is everything. Melancholics will really read context into your statement that often simply is not there, they may infer intent that simply is not there, Phlegmatics may just agree to get you off their backs and quietly view you as a bother, employing a variety of non-confrontational avoidance tactics and sanguines will often fail to understand or engage with what you are saying as they turn and twist in creative exploration, often avoiding the uncomfortable. What tends to happen is that when people take a stand against Cholerics, they have become quite entrenched and are not willing to discuss it, some of this is self-protection and some of it is that they have lost the argument so many times that they no longer care for discussion at all and have now resolved to act as they wish. Your fire inspires the fire in other types so use your fire well.

Helping, supporting and acting upon what you perceive without really understanding how it will be perceived will often supply others with help and support that they are not ready for and so may be unable to benefit. Often if they do benefit from it, they really did not know that they did. How on earth can someone appreciate what they do not know and understand? It is impossible. You have to have relationships in which you talk and share your heart so that they understand where you are coming from and that is work and investment at a skill that Cholerics are particularly weak at. Remember that relationships are a collaboration and if you allow them or encourage them to be one sided, they will never work. Often the cracks and breakdowns will appear when things are already irreconcilable. Often people will only appreciate what they have lost when it is gone! In shorthand you have got to learn to communicate and to listen to where the thinking of the other person is and, as with all of us, there is often a gulf between our actions, our perception and thinking. We will all spend a lifetime working at this one. As we communicate and learn the skill of communication this gulf will, more often than not, become more and more clear to us. The truly courageous recognise this and work at dealing with it. In the short term, most people find it much easier to employ some variation of avoidance strategies. The Choleric will, however, often make a scene to distract themselves from what has become glaringly apparent.

If you are in a relationship with a Choleric learn to empathise with them and try to understand and notice what they do. Their way of showing appreciation is in action, they want to ensure that the fruits are picked and that they and others benefit. So, they will often steam ahead dealing with things that you are still unaware of. Part of the difficulty is attaching the best interpretation to what they do in order that you begin to see what they are actually doing. Sometimes you have to learn to force them to talk and explain themselves, however this is not what a Choleric usually does and so there may be lots of tantrums on the way. But once they begin to understand that it will make them better at getting things done, with time they will embrace it.

Mornings are usually a bad time to get in the way of Cholerics, it is the wrong time to try to talk or do things that do not fit with their natural pattern. Often the pressure felt to get things done is greatest in the morning and if this is thwarted, they will feel frustrated throughout the day. Think of a train running down the hill, get out of the way and allow the momentum to spend itself before engaging. The time may vary, so watch and study them and see what that time is. It is best to help them if you want to engage so that the pressure to get things done subsides. However often you may find that having finished one thing they may merely start another, but there is only so much fuel in all of us and so watch for the slowdown in momentum. Insist on sitting over a cup of tea, water or a snack and chatting. But remember that once they have accepted or understood your point of view, they will usually want to act on it quickly. It really is worth taking the time to understand them.

Learn to stand up to Cholerics. They will respect this. There are some things that you simply cannot give ground on for the sake of keeping the peace.

As a Choleric you have to be able to spot when someone is taking the time to work with you, and to work hard at responding appropriately.

In order for the relationship to succeed, they have to understand what your broad intent and direction are and to share in at least some of your vision. If you learn to hear what is really happening with them, then things stand a fighting chance. Listen and ensure that they understand where you are coming from.

If you are tired, stressed, emotionally imbalanced and frustrated you will tend to be incredibly self-centred, selfish and insensitive. Often, this is because your reflexive response is to protect the fuel source which fire so desperately depends upon. You are caught in a purely visceral, unarticulated awareness of your own weakness that has bypassed any pause for introspective examination or inner dialogue. When you find yourself being automatically selfish or falling back on any of the other negative attitudes I have just mentioned, then step back, rest, clarify your intentions, look carefully to understand what must be done and what can be left, and work at connecting to the energy that will enable you to realign yourself.

When in love, you may have a tendency to give confusing signals. You will pursue the person or sometimes make your affections known, and at other times you will be short, cutting and sharp. You do not do vulnerability well.

Remember that the person who chooses you will have to be tough, caring and able to see beyond mere surface appearances.

If you are pursuing a Choleric, you will really need to be able to see beyond the outward appearances, and to learn to detect their deep feelings which gather below the surface, occasionally erupting like a volcano under the invisible build-up of subterranean pressures. That is just the way Cholerics are constructed and to reach them you have to look into the mouth of the volcano, which will often mean getting your hair singed. You just need to decide in advance whether you think it's worth the risk.

Cholerics - remember that you need to take time to communicate with those close to you to be sure that they understand you and you them. A really easy way of doing this is taking quality leisure time away with them. And it ensures that you take time to rest and recover actively.

Choleric Strategies

Full Steam Ahead! Take No Prisoners!

The favourite strategy of the Choleric is to steam ahead regardless of the consequences. To push on and to keep pushing. To fire off orders and to keep pressing on, driving towards the things that they perceive as important or necessary. As a Choleric you should ensure that the general situation maintains healthy diversity and flexibility for the next project, because if you exhaust your human and social resources on the current one, there will be nothing left in the pot for the next one. Remember the types from Know Yourself, there are two orientations, those who focus on the goal and destination (you are from this group) and those for whom the journey is the most important. The balance is somewhere in between these two positions. On a journey you must have stopping places, refuelling, resting places, times to recover from the pressure, times to drive on single-mindedly towards the goal, and times to give the scenery, the surroundings and the company their due. Journeys are just like this. Therefore, you have to take stock of the elements of the journey and learn to find a balance that you can work with and what is best for the group of people you are with.

Action Is Better Than Inaction

The other strategy of the Choleric is less of a strategy than a principle. Cholerics are more comfortable with action than inaction and frequently never learn that in creation something is always happening and that learning to let things take their natural course will often achieve a lot more than our rushed interventions. Also, sometimes the best actions are silence and inaction; these allow things to move on, and enable us to spot the moment when it is most beneficial to act. Stopping outward movement opens the way to inward movement. Contraction in the one direction leads you to expansion the other. Therefore, stilling your limbs and turning to silence will open up the inward chatter and movement. Both types of movement are necessary if we are to know ourselves. So, though this may be initially an uncomfortable skill for you to acquire, persisting in it will pay dividends. You will often realise later that you have underestimated the usefulness and benefits of silence, inaction and introspection until much later, when the hidden treasures gained become apparent. This is a constant theme across all the types; that in the skills and dispositions that we lack, there are great gifts to be found, if we set out courageously and steadily with the determination necessary to acquire them.

The Choleric in Love

A Choleric in love is a thing to behold. They either draw you in clearly and hold you close to their hearts with warmth and a sense of protection, or alternatively, they offer up mixed messages. They make it clear that they like you and then lash out or the consistency with which their irritated, irascible attentions land upon you lets you know that they either really hate you and find you irritating or that they are really interested. Take your bets and stick your hand in the lion's mouth and just refuse to take it out until you secure the love prize. This Choleric will maul you and the risks and trials which you were able to bear earns their respect, and they may then direct all their love deservingly and unequivocally toward you. If they really hate you, well, you will just get a mauling (and a measure of their respect). However, know that with this type of Choleric there will be lots of fireworks. A Choleric in love must respect you and you have to earn it. But Cholerics are surprising, as often it may seem transactional, they let you know clearly that they are interested, accept your interests in a matter of a fact manner and in the same vein let you know that you are together. They may show intense passion and love and then demand their own space. Yes, it is a bit like playing Russian Roulette, and the same Choleric may manifest all these possibilities in the space of a single week... Good luck!

Oh, and Cholerics in love! You know yourselves.

The Choleric Friend

You will be organised, told what to do, have to deal with brutal honesty and you will certainly know where you stand. You will also have to deal with someone who is often multi-tasking, who will be with you and will sound out what is going on in their lives with you, often with a few recriminations and a dislike of your disagreement. On the other hand they respect you speaking your mind and though they will react badly to your disagreements, in the medium to long term they tend to get over it. Fire flares up and settles down, do not get too caught up with the flare ups. Since we are attracted to our opposites, Cholerics often end up with close friends with very different if not opposite qualities. With a Choleric you need to listen and to guard your space firmly, strongly and fiercely if necessary. Cholerics, like fire, are naturally invasive so maintaining your boundaries is essential if you desire a collaborative healthy relationship. Since disagreement with a Choleric usually means that they will think that you are not that smart, you must be firm and clear in your disagreements. When necessary, allow them to know where you stand and over time to learn to work with that. Afterwards you must give them time and bear in mind that frequently you will not get an acknowledgement of your correctness or an apology. This is because Cholerics usually find this difficult to do verbally but will make amends in action, which means a lot more to a Choleric. You will have to keep your eyes open in order to observe and to understand the way in which Cholerics handle situations.

Relationships take time and we must learn to work with people according to their types. We cannot decide how they should be, because people and situations are what they are. The use of the word **should** denotes that the thing didn't happen. If we wish to have fulfilling relationships, then we must treat people according to their actual natures. With Cholerics you must quietly stand your ground, without becoming drawn into the spontaneous momentary flareups. With Cholerics respect is something that is earned. There will be difficulties in the friendship, you may often disagree, argue and stop speaking to each other, but the relationship will possess depth and Cholerics will come to your aid and defence. They are fiercely loyal and will break friendships because of disloyalty, they will support you, often rushing to your aid.

As a Choleric you must have friends who go that extra mile with you, learn to listen. Realise how you are and see yourself from the points of view of others. Yours is not the only valid standpoint.

Some helpful tips (Learn to listen):

1. Remember you can be quite prickly. That is just the way you are wired.

2. Listen, give your friends space, and if you really care about the relationship learn to offer the olive branch first! Yes, I know that is difficult;

3. Take some time out with your friends and give them all of your attention when you are with them. Be absolutely present with them;

4. Remember 2+7=9, 3+3+3=9, 5+4=9, 8+1=9, 3+6=9, 10-1=9, 21-12=9, etc. There are many

ways to get to the same point and many different ways to view the world and yours is certainly not the only one;

5. Sometimes when you win, you really lose!

Invest in Relationships

Cholerics have an eye on the future and the now, as the now relates to the future. The past for them is only as it relates to the future and so they dwell there extremely fleetingly. As a result, they tend not to appreciate your reminding them of the past, and especially not their historical failings. Cholerics need friends who provide them with other views. Melancholics focus upon the past and the future and have difficult dwelling in the present. Phlegmatics dwell in the present and the past and have difficulty with the future. Sanguines dwell in the present and relate to the future as it relates to the present. You need relationships that give you access to other ways of seeing the world, for your focus leaves you blind to modes of seeing that are not natural to you.

As a Choleric your strengths dictate your weaknesses and so success will come by accepting what your strengths and weaknesses are and acting accordingly. Because your attentions are so focussed you need trusted relationships, which give you access to other ways of seeing things. For self-mastery and success this is the price. So, investing in and learning to develop relationships is an absolutely necessary skill for a Choleric.

If you are not a Choleric yourself, but you have relationships with Cholerics, hold the best opinion you can of them and make excuses for their prickly ways. Focus on what they do, and you will see that they will tend to support you. However, when a Choleric is badly out of balance you need to protect yourself. Hold a safe distance and let them know that you love them unconditionally but that you have boundaries, so that they understand how to approach you. An out of balance Choleric, will tend to be incredibly self-centred and that is how they are made. Give them time. The fuel eventually burns out and meltdown will most likely follow soon after, and then you can help to pick up the pieces, but even then, ensure that you maintain your boundaries. With everyone, but especially with Cholerics, boundaries must be maintained.

Remember that fire is fire. It warms and it heats, it brings change, it burns and it destroys. To benefit from fire and to be safe from its harm, we must have discipline and wisdom with it.

The Choleric at Work

Get to the point and get it done. What is the point of stretching it out? The job that goes on forever without end is a frustrating and unrewarding one.

Since Cholerics need variety, challenge and results, they incline towards that which challenges them, which demands resourcefulness and which produces tangible results, in order to keep them interested and motivated. Gathering people, motivating them and driving towards a goal are the kind of thing that Cholerics really love. If the role does not offer these opportunities together with the prospect of clear and rapid results, it will tend to be very frustrating for a Choleric. The other danger a Choleric must be careful of, is drowning out the creativity of those working with them. Learn to harness the creativity and genius of the other types and do not stamp this out in order to make them an extension of your Choleric will, in order to complete the project. The genius of leadership lies in the capacity to harness the genius of others.

Three Ways of Dealing with Extended Projects

Take Breaks

I have to repeat this. Take breaks and ensure that you pace yourself. Cholerics burnout because they will push and push and push. Learn to pace yourself and to avoid burning out those around you. Leisure in which you can forget yourself is absolutely necessary for a Choleric.

The Impossible - Patience: 5 Ways to be Patient

Nothing is perhaps more frustrating for a Choleric than being patient. They want the result, and they want it now! One way to deal with this is to work at achieving things in an almost effortless fashion. This will take timing, restraint, insight and wisdom. It will force you to look below the surface and see the inner rhythms of things. It will entail learning to act when the action will have the greatest effect and patience will emerge somewhere along the way as you learn to do this. For a Choleric this will be difficult.

This other aspect of patience is to be certain of a good outcome. Practise expecting good, healthy outcomes and work actively and steadily to build them. The Sufis have a saying, "Allah is to the servant as the servant's opinion is of Him.". This is the true foundation of patience. Our anxiety at the outcome is often blinding, knowing that good will eventually result from a good intention and consistent, balanced, appropriate action, frees us to commit to working towards the goal in a manner that encourages a good outcome. The acceptance of fate's decree is not the same as having a fatalistic attitude; it entails a conscious realisation that you are not excluded from the unfolding path of the decree, on the contrary. The interwoven threads of the web of destiny that encompass the entirety of existence enfold you too, and you act in accordance with your part and your place in the scheme of things. Your willingness and your consistency will bear its fruit, though the results are often unexpected and sometimes you may fail spectacularly, but with hindsight you find you will have won more often than you lost:

1. Watch the rhythms, timing and movements of things and projects, learn the rhythms and phases and learn to work with them;

2. Do not pick an unripe fruit. Learn to encourage things to come to their natural fruition and practise recognising the signs that this has happened;

3. Have a good opinion of the creation. Expect good to come out of even disaster. Learn to recognise actions, things and times that are pregnant with healthy possibilities and study how to encourage them;

4. Expect from people only what they are capable of doing. If you get people to go beyond their usual limits, you should know that this isn't what will normally happen. Construct the project based upon what you know that they will do as opposed to what you think they should do. Successes tend to make people a little more adventurous. Increase the possibilities by encouraging people with minor successes;

5. Learn to body breathe as babies do. It centres us and this makes it easier to deal with anxiety, fears and anger. By being calmer, you will be much less impatient. The practice of Yoga is a great way to return to body breathing.

Cholerics at Play

Cholerics have to win. More often than not, play will be organised so that it fulfils a purpose. Strip away the need to always win at games, for in this arena winning often means losing in the long run. Conserve the will. Will is energy and so it is not limitless.

The types in whom the characteristics of flexibility, intuition and immersion in the journey rather than the goal dominate - Phlegmatics and Sanguines - will play solely for the fun of it. Play is for them true leisure, which gives the benefit of relaxation, energetic renewal and fun. Win or lose they will enjoy themselves. This is not at all true for the Choleric. However, it is a very useful ability to acquire. Goal orientation and exertion, takes its energetic toll. Being process oriented or enjoying the journey rather than focusing upon the goal, brings an abandon and free spiritedness not natural to the Choleric. With this abandon there comes a renewal in leisure which is impossible to experience without it. The Choleric would benefit immensely from this. This is an ability to play without concern for the outcome, the Choleric propensity to win will then emerge anyway, but with a casual, joyful freedom that allows others to be and enjoy themselves.

This is best achieved by getting out of the way. Cholerics, this is a time to step aside and let the Sanguines and the Phlegmatics take charge. Learn from them, observe and imitate. Learning to find this abandon and joy in the texture of the journey, will enable you to learn the skill of making the journey fun and this is an essential skill in leadership. This is one of those times when letting go of the reins actually teaches better leadership. We need each other and there are important life lessons that each type has for the others. Learning how to benefit from the unique perspectives of others and the patterns of the other types is one of the most valuable lessons in wisdom that we can learn.

The Choleric Student

Burnout

The greatest dangers for the Choleric are always burnout and stress. Your need to fill time with activity, interests and achievement must be balanced by rest, leisure and relaxation. To keep the fire going you require fuel and renewal, without which you will just repeatedly crash. Structure your time and give to each part its due. Burnout means that you must rest, or at least, slow down.

If you become irritable, red faced or angry, with an unsettling feeling that won't go away, and that your right eye is twitching uncontrollably, or that you are constantly frustrated and perhaps teary, then you are most likely exhausted and drained. Take a swim, a rest or a long walk. Strip the activity back to what really must be done, and if that is too much, then cut it back some more. Be ruthless in stripping things back and refilling your energetic tanks. Having massages, staring into wood fires and taking saunas will also help.

Avoid the temptation to keep pushing ahead with the aid of stimulants. Stimulants feed on energetic reserves. When your reserves are low this type of strategy is a suicidal one. Drink lots of water, eat well and rest.

Remember, that as a Choleric you want to keep busy, to push ahead and to achieve. Willpower is in plentiful supply and you may literally run yourself into the ground. Being stubborn and wilful, you are in danger of taking on too much and not giving yourself enough time to recover. Being patient is usually difficult for Cholerics and as a result, Cholerics will tend to throw more and more at the same problem, instead of watching carefully, understanding, and opting to expend as little as possible to achieve as much as possible. Cholerics feel pressure to get the job done. The Choleric student will fill their time with activities and stands in danger of exhausting their energetic resources and, if left unchecked, they eventually succeed in exhausting themselves utterly. Then they will beat themselves up, accusing themselves of being lazy and dragging themselves back to the grindstone repeatedly, despite it being clear to others that the only solution is rest and relaxation. More especially when tired, the Choleric may lack focus and get involved in a wide variety of things, dissipating their energy and burning themselves out.

Eight Tips for Pacing Yourself

The Eight Tips:

1. Do not commit to anything too easily. Resist closing down your options at the beginning, and ensure that what you involve yourself in is in your best interests, fits with your general plans and that there are sufficient resources to get the job done. If not, just leave it alone and move on;

2.   Have a rhythm with a timetable that you can stick to. Ensure that rest, exercise and relaxation are present in sufficient doses, or you will become exhausted and imbalanced;

3.   Only use the natural tactic of constantly battering the wall to tear it down, when there is absolutely no other option. This tactic expends a lot of energy and sometimes other more subtle tactics get the job done with much greater ease. If unavoidable, then ensure that afterwards there is sufficient rest and leisure to fully recuperate;

4.   Get a phlegmatic friend and observe how they do things. See what lessons you can learn;

5.   Celebrate your victories and those of your friends. Make it leisurely;

6.   Discuss things aloud with yourself, and keep a check on what is happening in your life. Talk aloud to yourself whilst in the bath or sitting alone. Realign and readjust regularly;

7.   When you get it wrong, laugh about it. Step back and adjust. It is important to laugh it off;

8. Do not try to be patient. That is going to give you hypertension. Focus upon rhythm and acting with timing in order to achieve effortlessly. This will bring you the benefits of patience without you having to sweat about being patient.

Choleric Learning and Study Style

Cholerics learn by doing. They have to be active and what they learn has to engage with the real world. They come to conclusions quickly and tend to learn fast. Often much too fast. Remember that learning is like eating, if you don't chew your food you will end up with indigestion. You've got to chew your knowledge so that it digests into you and a firm understanding eventually becomes yours. Make yourself look at what you learn from more than one angle until that which you have learned becomes digested allowing you to use it and understand it well. Diagrams are good for you; quick, short notes, audio clips and even the occasional video. Another way to enhance your learning experience is to get a project going; presenting and sharing what you have learned. This forces you to digest it, which then ensures that you have really grasped the subject in a manner that results in something tangible.

Set up mind-maps of what you know, if you do not know what mind-maps are, get online and look at Tony Buzan's work on mind-maps. There's a load of free software out there;

Put reminders and titbits of information on the walls of the places where you do things in order to make memorising easy;

Take breaks on the hour - just walk around, do press-ups, squats, sit-ups, have water and then come back to what you were doing. If you choose exercise, set a number for the day and when you break keep chipping away at the number that you have allotted yourself;

Repeat things aloud to yourself;

Do presentations with a study partner and be mutually reflective about what was presented.

Choleric Decision-Making

Choleric decision-making can be described as quick and decisive. Their decisions flow like quicksilver, things are weighed up with a rapidity that conceals the steps in the decision-making process (most usually all their own). Cholerics just know, they know quickly, and they rapidly move on to action. Their certainty can be unnerving, or alternatively, confidence inspiring.

They find it difficult to explain their decisions to others, it is often the case that Cholerics will not waste the time to explain their actions since they 'know' that they are right, and they just want to get on with it. It is really so obvious to them that if you can't see it, why on earth should they waste unnecessary time explaining it? You must be really stupid if you can't see it! Once the decision is made then the pressure is on to act. For there is now pressure to commit to a course of action and so get the job done.

Since Cholerics are usually right, they are often unable to improve on how they make decisions, especially as things tend to be black and white for them. it is either correct or it is not. The course of action is either the correct one or it is not. This is because the dry types lack flexibility in response and need to commit to a course of action. This means that when a Choleric makes a decision, options are rapidly eliminated in order to push on to a decision which will result in action. Any exploration of options serves only to facilitate the process of elimination, and to arrive at a quick decision. Elegance and articulate expression in the solution are really of secondary importance, if accorded any importance at all! If a Choleric consults your opinion they will often cut you off mid-sentence the instant they feel that what you have to say is not going to be part of the solution. Melancholics and Phlegmatics will find them rude, whilst Sanguines will think that they miss so much; Sanguines love to explore and then to put together an elegant artistic response to the problem. Cholerics also tend to only want the information they ask for, and no more. Melancholics and Sanguines will want to give context and options, infuriating the Choleric, whilst the Choleric's bluntness infuriates them.

Learning the difficult task of explaining your Choleric actions to others is dealt with in the next section, Choleric Communication.

Choleric Communication

Listen, For God's Sake!

This is the most difficult skill for the Choleric to learn. As soon as you think that you have grasped what is being said the Choleric in you switches off. This will often mean that you have listened but not heard what is really being said. It is important to grasp where people really are, Phlegmatics are masters of this skill. Phlegmatics listen, they really listen and if you wish to learn how to listen, then learn this from a Phlegmatic. Phlegmatics and Cholerics often have some traits in common and there is much that they can learn from each other. These dynamics often make relationships between the two types difficult. Until you are able to spot the similarities and grasp the nature of your differential motivations, there will be considerable difficulty, but that is part of the challenge. You both will often fail to share your thoughts, though for vastly different reasons. Convincing a Phlegmatic to work with you will be hard work and forcing them to do so by constant badgering is not the best way to get them to work with you. You will have to befriend the Phlegmatic in order to get the best results. Remember that they are water and so they are masters at slipping through your fingers in a non-confrontational manner.

Another practice is to listen and to ask questions that help you to really understand where people are coming from. Learning to ask the questions that make clear not only what people appear to be saying, but also how they feel. The way that people feel about things dictates how they will behave in relation to it over long periods of time. It is therefore important that you grasp how they feel and what they want. As a Choleric you will have to begin by actively getting people to talk and learning to shut up whilst allowing them to continue talking and helping them along as is required. As you become better at it then you will be able to help them to get talking with less effort and relying less on the sound of your own voice. To do this you will have to use phlegmatic strategies. You will find that as you learn to do so you will also become much more flexible.

Whilst listening internally look into your heart. This will make you more aware of your inner feelings. Connect to your breathing and let your breaths sink deep into your abdomen as a baby breathes. Become aware of the soles of your feet and this will help to keep you grounded and calm. The fire wants to leap into action, but what you need to do is to just let the flame calmly and effortlessly burn so that it merely warms up the atmosphere. Keep a glass of water nearby and take a sip from time to time as you feel like it.

Doodle and sketch, keeping notes of what is being said so that you can easily return to relevant points. With time and practice you will get better at it all. Just listen for God's sake!

Four Points to Successful Communication

1. Work at being interested in the point of view of others. Work at finding points of interest in the conversation. It may be an

interest in what really motivates them, what really works for them or alternatively what doesn't. Work out their personality type from the conversation. Be interested in the dynamics of your communication, work out what works and what doesn't. Just find a way to keep your interest going. I often struggle with this myself and as a young man acquired many enemies by failing to do just this. You don't have to agree or disagree with people but they each bring a unique perspective into the world and being interested helps us to derive some benefit from it. Life is study and it is the transformation of our behaviour, attitudes and perspectives which offer the greatest scope for change, wisdom and insight. Learning to be interested in the perspective of others saves time and can often offer unbelievable benefits. Along the way, you'll have to conquer your boredom, but that is not the other person, but rather our own attitude to the situation.

2. Fire is explosive, the energy of Cholerics is rapid, like the staccato rhythm of machine gun fire. Others find this challenging and will defend themselves against what they may often experience as an assault on their senses and themselves. Though Cholerics

often do not intend this, it is unfortunately how they may be experienced. The colder types - Melancholics and Phlegmatics - have to be coaxed out of their caves and this just sends them running deeper inside for cover. Fire is active and to communicate you have to shift between the active and the passive or receptive energies. If you take control, then the other will have to become receptive and in so doing, fail to bring forth their treasures. Fire must become water in order to embrace the communication of others. Visualise water and become receptive. Smoothen your energy and attitude so that grace and gentleness emerge, this will help you to get others talking to you and you will not startle them into retreat. This will be incredibly difficult unless you are a Choleric-Phlegmatic, but if treasure was easily gained then it wouldn't be a treasure, would it?

3. Do not always be swift to punish stupidity. Let things take their course and observe what is happening. Sometimes stupidity turns out not to be so stupid after all, and if something really is stupid, it speaks quite clearly for itself, hence saving you the extra trouble required to force the point home.

4. You know your thoughts by doing. Verbalising them is usually the most difficult skill for you. They tend to come out jumbled. It will take practice and an understanding audience to get over the initial hurdles as you learn to deal with communicating your decisions. You just have to keep hurdling the path over the obstacles. You will also have to spend time alone; walking or swimming is a good way for you to become more acquainted with your inner workings.

Silence

Learn to use silence. Silence is usually seen as passive and receptive, and it is predominantly these things but silence can also be active. All Cholerics know that when you ask a difficult question, shut up and leave the pressure to mount. Study silence, use silence and make silence your friend.

Waiting

The companion of silence is waiting. Wait to see what is below the surface of the lake. Wait to see who will act first. Wait to see who is wisest. Wait to see how people really are. Wait to understand the situation and know what is possible, what cannot be done and what will be achieved only with great difficulty. Active waiting really helps you to know what you are getting into. If you want to win, learn to wait. Action is like lightning and waiting is often like the rain. Act without hesitation and wait for the moment.

Communicating Choleric Decisions

A Choleric once commented,

"I always find group/team meetings so frustrating... I find others take far too long to reach decisions, and meetings and solutions drag on... if my solution is not accepted or if it is not my area of expertise... in order to control my frustrations, I turn to doodling to pass the time whilst they decide on what to do!

Once I have something or a process set in my head, I'm so rigid with it that I dislike explaining myself or overcomplicating my explanations! However, when I take the time to explain I find that others give me ideas or easier solutions that I would never have thought of!"

I have included this because it summarises the Choleric communication difficulty and the benefits of being able to communicate.

Cholerics very quickly chart the path of ideas to outcomes with instinctive swiftness, for that is essential to the role that they play. What

Cholerics must realise is that once action is committed to, time, resources and emotional energy are spent and these cannot be replaced, for each of these things are only spent once. Robust solutions that engage teams requires that the team take possession of the course of action i.e. if the team views the solution as their own then they pour even more of their energy and emotional resources into it and you will not have to do so much marshalling together, for they will then be self-motivated. This will engage a set of skills that the Choleric does not naturally engage. The communication required will be two-fold:

1. Their communication to you – learning how to understand what they see. This means that you will have to suspend agreement and disagreement in order to hear what they are really saying. This is the skill of facilitating the expression and development of ideas of others. This requires the deployment of empathy, which is absolutely essential to the development and expression of mercy and compassion. This allows you to listen to others and benefit from their insights. However, the Choleric need to drive on to action and the natural impatience of this type make this a very difficult approach.

2. Your communication to them - learning how to become aware of what is implicit in your arguments and decisions, to accept challenges to your decisions and thinking, and when necessary, to revise your opinion. Working with others to create facilitative environments encourages others to offer you reciprocal support in the communication of your positions in response to the empathy you have shown. For Cholerics this takes a committed group, in which trust, collaboration and mutual development are the culture.

I am suggesting that this will not be an easy challenge. You will need a supportive environment to take this one on. For others will have to be willing and able to see past any hint of anger, frustration and intolerance. You will all have to commit to being better at what you do and the willingness to take a more difficult road in the short to medium term in order to gain greater mastery in the long term. The thing about skills acquired is that they are yours and yours for life.

Five Steps to Effective Decision Making for the Choleric

The Choleric problem is surely not making decisions. The Choleric problem is the quality of the decisions due to the habitual hastiness of the type.

1. Cholerics focus upon the goal rather than the experience of the journey. The journey to the goal must also be considered and it is ignored at your peril and at the peril of those around you. Cholerics are often blind to this aspect. We must hold over ourselves an obligation to be merciful to ourselves and to each other and part of this mercy is the consideration of the nature and texture of the journey. Speaking figuratively, consider natural stopping places, avoid difficult terrain, ensure that the terrain is rich in fruits, seek places to celebrate, seek company that brings pleasure and always balance work and pleasure, always. Without the above, journeys or projects become unnecessarily difficult. What holds the project together in balance is rhythm, the rhythmic balance of work and rest; indulgence and sacrifice; relaxation and activity. With rhythm we can keep going on, we have to consider our natural resources and there will come times for assessment, a knowledge of the signs of stress and the approach of collapse, and a knowledge of how to proceed healthily with balance. When we embark upon a project or choose

a goal consider: the experience and texture of the journey and compassion for ourselves and for others.

2. Projects take resources. Consider goodwill, mutual support, allies, finances or wealth, time, tasks, recovery and renewal and any other matters. These are all important factors. Do not squander them. The longer the project the more stress it places upon your resources and the more important rhythm becomes. Factor these elements into your planning and develop relationships in which you can talk about them with people you can trust and who possess the relevant experience.

3. Everything has a natural rhythm of expansion and contraction, rising and falling, opening and closing, plenty and scarcity, etc. We must develop a grasp of these rhythms, for they are akin to breathing. Remember that whatever we are doing we must be prepared for these recurrent patterns. We must not expect existence to make exceptions for us. The Reality is The Reality and there is no altering it. Everything must submit to its order for they are all part of Reality. The more we harmonise the easier it gets. Difficulty and ease are also a reality and

natural rhythm; to expect them to be suspended for us is the height of self-delusion. Reality will break you and you cannot break The Real.

4. Work from a base and view it as your metaphorical kingdom. This could be your expertise, business, household or anything that fits the description. Your decisions affect your kingdom. Put into your kingdom more than you take out. Scout from it. Explore abroad with light forces. Venture out and return but remember that your kingdom is your kingdom and never destroy it, pillage its resources or fail to take care of it. If your kingdom is only you, then what is the use of a kingdom?

5. Cholerics are subject to deep anxieties and fears. Fire knows that it needs fuel. Acknowledge your anxieties and fears, they are not weaknesses. Weakness is to submit to the anxieties and fears without paying attention to the warnings they often convey. Make the best use of your fears and anxieties, when they are unfounded strengthen yourself by resisting them, and when they have a basis pay attention, ensuring that the questions they raise are dealt with or prepared for. To ignore them

is stupidity and to submit to them is weakness.

The Choleric Alone

Cholerics are people persons. Equipped for the role they naturally play they are wired to be in groups and so they usually find being with people energising. When in a state of imbalance, they often display a compulsive tendency to seek company. This can be a good thing. However, where there is inner confusion or manifest emotional disturbance, then spending some time alone is required. The problem is that when painful feelings and memories come welling up from deep within, you react by burying them under a pile of activity. This merely defers the pain to another time and this pattern results in an accumulation of unresolved or undigested issues.

Cholerics require time alone, some of this should be spent remaining still and some should be spent being active. They usually require an activity that holds their attention, gardening, bonsai tending, painting, playing a musical instrument, or some similar activity which holds and focuses the attention in a calming and soothing manner; swimming, jogging and walking will also serve the purpose. Whatever is indulged in should be centring and continue long enough with sufficiently gentle and effortless focus to cause the chattering brain to be overcome by the heart which reflects. Once the brain is silenced, your reflections will rise up as if from the bottom of an ocean and you will be buoyed up in them. It is here that things will become clarified, you will become aware of contradictions, you will see the connections between the seemingly unrelated and meanings will come running to you. For you are part of a great ocean and as you become aware of it, you increasingly shed the diseases of isolation and dislocation as your true self seeks out integrity and unity. It is here that the search begins for that which you did not even know you were looking for; and the Sufis are the guides to these places. It takes at least 45 minutes to begin to open these aspects of yourself. If you wish to cry then cry, to laugh then laugh, once you find yourself at the shores of this ocean then swim, do not hold on to anything, just swim. Man was made for this swimming. This is a necessary part of man's natural form. Today we are trying to introduce mindfulness and pseudo-spirituality as technological responses to this natural human need. It is feared that once man has tasted and drank from this Ocean, he will have tasted genuine freedom and our modern world will be revealed as an open prison. The Ocean is within you and solitude helps you to find it and Cholerics are utterly in need of finding the ocean, for without it there is no hope of contentment.

Eight Uses of Being Alone

1. Knowing yourself and the clarification of your thoughts;

2. Stilling your being and getting out of your head;

3. Shedding the turmoil - a smoke screen for internal pain and conflict - that Cholerics often seek;

4. Getting away from the compulsive need to organise and marshal people and things;

5. Crying and letting things go. States that you may be embarrassed to let people see. These are part of the human form, but we don't take people into the toilet with us, do we? Go out alone and lick your wounds;

6. Getting a break from irritating people. Ask for some alone time;

7. Before a great challenge it is sometimes good to take some time alone, with the universe. Know that it is the continuous

act of the Generous Creator, who is not off in the sky somewhere creating but is the very force, energy and impulse from Whom it all pours forth. Stand alone, and we are never alone, watch the challenge in your mind's eye, ask for victory, release the fears of losing, breathe into the kidneys, let the neck sink, connect the feet to the earth, see yourself upon your victory and know that win or lose, live or die your victory is truly this moment, in which you stood alone with The Force that moves every event, you connected and tasted something of your secret. Then go forward and fight as you have never fought, with every ounce of your being, as has never ever been seen in the universe and will never ever again be seen;

8. When you have poured out your being in a challenge, sit alone in the aftermath. Return to the place of aloneness that you tasted, relax your kidneys, sink your breath to the soles of your feet, smile inside and say thank you.

Five Ways to Make the Experience of Unwellness More Interesting

Illness is irritating. There is so much to do, and it just gets into the way. However, if we do not acknowledge that most illness arises from the contradictions and lack of balance in our lives then it will all just happen repeatedly. We must see illness as a messenger and pay attention to the message.

Five ways to make illness more interesting:

1. Reflect upon how you got ill. If you reflect upon how you got ill, it will inevitably lead to more questions. If you start with why, you will inevitably get it wrong. Stay calm, reflect upon the 'how' and leave the 'why' to present itself. Good idea to keep a notebook while you're at it, if you can;

2. Sleep and sleep and sleep. Once you have the energy you will start to dream. Then try to remember your dreams;

3. Learn to let people look after you. Practise being like water, imagine water, taste it, feel it around you, feel it quench your thirst, remember the sweetest water you ever tasted and relax. Smile when people help you and be like a cat, if you like what they do, encourage it and let

them know, and if you don't, gently pull away. There is so much to learn from cats. Ensure that you take what you learn into your everyday life. You don't always have to be active to get things done;

4. Gently explore your body from the inside with your conscious mind. Imagine cool rainwater wash through each places as it comes into focus. Don't force anything. Stop when you get tired, then sleep;

5. Listen to and observe people. They will talk to you, so ask gentle questions. Don't defend yourself if you don't like the answers. Try to see things from their perspective and gently form a picture of yourself through the eyes of others. You don't have to like the picture. We often don't. This may help you to get a better grasp on how you got to where you are. Remember that blame isn't going to help anyone. Understanding how what you did helped you to get to where you are means that you can do something about what YOU do.

Choleric Impulses

Driving forward towards a goal is where you feel alive and valued. You need to have things to do and this will often define you. Where

Sanguines are driven by passion, you seem driven by drive itself. This tendency to activity and a sense of unease with inactivity often characterises you and may even at times tyrannise you. This sets up one of life's great lessons for you, the Choleric, for without being able to stand down from the drive when appropriate this becomes the tyrannical drive which will drive you to imbalance and illness, as well as to success and high repute. Remember that our greatest gifts become our greatest weaknesses if used inappropriately.

You can drive forward at incredible cost, it is as if your psyche has such a high level of command in subjecting your body to the will to drive that you are often unaware of the ultimate price of your desire for success and for winning (at all costs!). Whereas the Sanguine has stamina, you have the compulsion to act. A single-mindedness which seems to bend the very fabric of your reality. This is the dry principle in action; focussed, inflexible and transforming. It dominates and shapes your life, and you shouldn't give it up for anything. However, there is a lesson you must learn having been blessed with this gift of yours. This lesson is that the container which carries the drive requires care to maintain the drive. You are often in danger of completely exhausting and destroying that container, whether it be your body, your team or any other situation which provides the support and context within which you pursue your goals. The truth is that the drive is part of you and when out of balance you destroy yourself.

There are times when you will look for a project just to make life tolerable and then immerse yourself in activity in order to escape your everyday problems. This is a coping strategy, and it really isn't a way to live your life. So, if you persistently find yourself repeating this pattern, then admit that you have a problem that needs to be addressed. Often the solutions are completely beyond your skill set, but that is exactly where the learning opportunities dwell. Oh, Choleric, though you are the superhero of the types, you too are in need of others and their varieties of natural genius. So, seek help and keep seeking help until you find it. It will be here that you come face to face with the Choleric's hatred of vulnerability, which is the underbelly of your mighty gift of impulsivity. We are all given great gifts, but we are also tested by their consequences!

You are wired with quick, incisive, staccato rhythm judgement. You evaluate in an instant - a signature expression of the impulsiveness of fire. It burns through and clarifies. You tear through the layers to get at what really matters, evaluating on the basis of what you want to achieve. It is fiery, revealing, penetrating and relentless. It leaps over the ground in hungry pursuit of the next objective. Unceasing, unsettled and restless. How does one live with this? Well, you have lived with it your whole life! There are times when you must ground yourself, within the company of those who work from a very different impulse and whose judgement you have come to respect. If there are no such persons in your circle then you really need to get out more. Then there are times that you must learn to ground this with leisure and meditation that renews you from deep within. For fire to keep burning it needs fuel and you need to come up for air, so to speak. Without finding this equilibrium you will burn out.

From a place of stillness this fiery, active and achieving nature will be able to see, re-evaluate and recalibrate. A place of stillness can help you to eventually see how to achieve and move forward with less effort, but you will have to invest in developing this aspect of yourself. From here you may learn the arts of activation, maturation and completion through one project, and then just waiting and watching for the next big undertaking to arrive, whilst you integrate and assimilate the lessons of the previous task into your being. Each project should bring greater maturity and understanding, without this we often relive the same dysfunctional patterns. Movement and stillness, and action and reflection, are inseparable siblings and we must learn to live in equilibrium with them all. Therefore, the word for today is *balance*.

As we have seen, a key aspect of your impulsive nature is that fire illuminates and clarifies. With fire we refine iron and derive steel, and it is with fire that we light the fires and lamps that give light in the darkness. It is a mark of the Choleric impulse to say that which must be said, and that being the case, will usually find it unbearable to remain silent in the face of a perceived injustice. What you do with this one is up to you. Remember that every impulse is precisely that, but appropriateness should determine how we react.

Summary

Now we have completed our journey of exploration around the majestic creature that is the pure Choleric. Have the insights and discoveries been helpful? I hope that the tools and techniques prove useful and that you'll be able to improve on them. By now, you should have a more confident hold on the dynamics of being choleric. Every strength by its nature exposes a weakness and often weaknesses can be turned into strengths. I am sure that you will work away at this. Remember that an important lesson throughout this journey is the importance of mastering the art of propriety by considering the context, our impulses, natural strategies and the subtle nuances of the situation. This hones wisdom and it is wisdom that tends to underpin the art of the apparently effortless success. Remember that your focus is legendary, so when you find it wavering, remember that focus requires energy and energy requires periodic rest and relief. When your focus is waning try rest rather than forcing yourself and doubling down! An oft-repeated piece of advice to you throughout this book has been to remember that the journey itself is important to many of the denizens to be found within the ecosystem of types so please, please, remember to cater for them too, so that you can see the importance of the part that enjoyment of the journey brings to the final attainment of the goals you are striving to achieve.

Work with the way you are. Deepen your understanding of how you work and learn to deploy it well. You are just wired this way.

Succeed gloriously and fail gloriously and learn to make the most of both your failures and your successes.

> If you can meet with triumphs and disaster

> And treat these two imposters just the same

> If

> **Rudyard Kipling**

They are both to be studied and learned from.

Ok, now let us get down to looking at the combinations! There's no time to waste!

The Mixes

Introduction

In the Sufic understanding - which is according to the Qur'anic cosmology - existence is a oneness, which is unfolded to express the realities hidden within that Unity. Two primal realities appear from the Creational Unity; these are The Lawh - The Tablet - and The Qalam - The Pen. The Pen is often called Aql - Intellect. The Qalam writes upon The Lawh what will be, what is and what was. This means that the pattern of the creation is embedded within it and written upon it. The Lawh embodies the passive principle and The Qalam the active. The passive principle may also be viewed as the feminine archetype, and the active principle the masculine archetype. The feminine archetype gives form, continuity, connection, pattern, nourishes, it provides a repository and connects future, present and past in continuity, whilst the masculine archetype gives energy, separation and differentiation, movement and expression, spends energy like lightning, pierces realities and separates future, present and past, so that continuity proceeds in epochs. Since the entire creation is a consequence of The Divine Light of Command, everything contains everything else. The Masculine is in the Feminine and the Feminine within the Masculine, the Unity pours forth differentiated forms, expressing realities hidden within the Unity until the revelation of their appearance. Within the Lawh is established archetypal forms and then from this issues forth the unfolding of the possibilities implied within it in an unendingly varied and Divinely inspired order. The archetype of leaf is established and then all the infinite possibilities of leaf pour forth, no two leaves ever being identical!

The archetypal reality of The Feminine archetype expresses two fundamental potentialities: The Cold - the propensity to stillness - and The Wet - the propensity to flexibility, spreading and connection. At the same time, the Masculine archetype also expresses the two counterpart fundamentals of: The Hot - the propensity to movement and change – and The Dry – the propensity to rigidity and separation. The whole of the creation is shaped by the dance of attraction and involvement between these potentialities, timelessly tracing out unimaginable interlocking patterns of endless love and the burgeoning desire to be known that sing of the realities yet hidden within the Unity. These four potentialities dance forth the Elemental forms; The Wet and The Cold combine giving rise to Elemental Water; The Wet and The Hot combine giving rise to Elemental Air; The Hot and the Dry combine giving rise to Elemental Fire; and The Cold and the Dry combine giving rise to Elemental Earth. Here upon this loom are drawn the energetic skeins from which the vast designs of the universe are woven.

This provides a glimpse into the constructive and destructive dynamic of the interplay between the fundamental energetic forces at work in the restless ocean of this creation of which we ourselves are an inseparable expression, as reflected in our individual telltale permutations of the energetic dialectics by which we may come to identify ourselves and others. The possession of the capacity to employ this knowledge, enables you to predict the pattern of things and the broad patterns of events.

This gives rise to bio-types and each Elemental Form is expressed in you. The first provides the form within which the other three can express their energetic pattern through you. The major differences are made by the base Element and the secondary one. In this series we ignore the third and fourth ones for they do not make the most significant difference. As a result, there are three expressions of the Choleric in the Know Yourself method:

The Choleric-Melancholic; The Choleric-Phlegmatic; and the Choleric-Sanguine.

As a Choleric you express the Masculine Active principle, you should reflect upon this for it will help to make you more effective. The Feminine and Masculine must interact. The masculine cannot succeed without the feminine and vice versa. The successful Choleric must learn to develop or employ the necessary capacities. This discipline and awareness are essential for the development of the Choleric. Without this Cholerics tend to be self-centred and egotistical. For you to succeed the feminine nurturing must be accompanied by the masculine goal led activity, driving things to their destination must be accompanied by nurturing energies.

What Makes You YOU?

From your father you received a fiery live seed delivered in waters, much like a tadpole and from your mother you received a seed fixed in the earth of the womb and bathed in blood which is upon the pattern of Elemental Air. These two combined in the earth of the womb, giving birth to a unity possessing an animal spirit and a temperamental balance born of the combination of the two. Anyone who reflects upon this must know that this is more miraculous than alchemy. The body and appetites will be most shaped by this, then during the time of the quickening, a soul is delivered by the Angelic Messengers and fused with the living being in the womb. By then, the single-celled being has differentiated its potentialities into clear organic systems expressing the pattern of energies that result in the form we call human. The soul is placed upon the throne of the heart and is made to establish its rulership over this animal spirit by binding it to the animal spirit at the nodes or connections which are held open for exchange at particular organic systems and at particular junctions. These junctions are like doors in the old sense for the main doors would open into a chamber and then to another door, and it is here that the animal soul is bound to the Ruh -

the soul brought by the Angelic Messengers - this soul wants to ascend and the animal soul wants to descend, pulling us towards the earths and the heavens. From now on they are as one soul until the disintegrating severance of the greater death. For those who journey the path, know that the lesser death referred to by the Sufis subjugates the animal soul utterly to the Ruh, the knots untangle and the cord of the two becomes one. It is as if a new being of light is born, luminous and illuminating, this is the alchemy for which you were born and for which man was created. Those who arrive at this point only get there by The Real drawing them in by the irrepressible energy of longing, which the Sufis call Himma. Himma is a treasured force that if it possesses you, you must submit. It is a force that will smash you if you resist it, for it is The Source of All Reality drawing you to a conscious witnessing and tasting of Reality. Imagine the fiery live seed of the father, for which swimming is everything. You too must swim!

The combination of the spirits as one is what results in you. This knowledge of personality types gives a knowledge of your nature which cuts right through to the core and reveals to you the nature of what you are. Then you will truly begin to understand how to ride the being you have been given.

The Choleric Forest

The way to grasp the differences in Cholerics is to imagine a forest of pine trees, each pine tree is unique, but upon inspection you discover that all the pine trees can be separated into three distinct types. In the Know Yourself method you possess Master and Servant aspects of your temperamental mix. The Master is the seat within which the other Elemental types express themselves. In the case of Cholerics the Master is the Choleric and the Servant will be one of the other three types giving Choleric-Melancholic, Choleric-Phlegmatic and Choleric-Sanguine. We will only consider the second most important element since the others will not have as great an effect as the interaction of these two. As you become more familiar with your own inner workings you will begin to see for yourself how the other Servant aspects express themselves, especially how different circumstances change the way in which you tend to behave.

1. Choleric-Melancholic: The Choleric provides the basis and the melancholic traits serve the choleric impulses. This is a complementary mix, meaning that this

type's behaviour is consistent as the two types combine well;

2. Choleric-Phlegmatic: The Choleric provides the basis and the phlegmatic traits serve the choleric impulses. This is a non-complementary combination but it is one of the most consistent of the non-complementary mixes. The phlegmatic aspects are smoothly expressed but not always in ways that are predictable;

3. Choleric-Sanguine: This is the hottest and most volatile of all the types. The Choleric provides the basis and the windy changeable sanguine traits are employed to serve the fiery choleric impulses. This is a hot dominant, exceedingly active and changeable type;

The Uniqueness of Each One of You

We are unique. Each person is an event that will never ever be repeated. The endless stream of patterned variables pouring out of reality without end, in each unique moment of time, strikes each thing with its own resounding sound. We don't have to try to be unique, that is the very peak of ignorance, the obvious truth of which is that it will always result in a banal sameness. You only have to let yourself be yourself but that is a process of emergence, study and an uncovering of your nature and refining of it. It is the endless revealing of the beauty of the gemstone as we cut, polish and uncover what is actually there, for what is not within the gemstone cannot by any stretch of the imagination be truly added to it. We have natural strengths and deficiencies, in us some things are absent, some things weakly represented and some plentiful and overflowing. Often we have to cut back the excess and strengthen the deficient. We have to recognise what may be absent and lean upon those who have it. All of this is the work of uncovering, cutting and polishing the unique event that is you or me. Accepting our limitations is a great strength for we are then freed to deal with ourselves as we are, rather than as we think we should be. We can cut through the nonsense and illusion to deal with what we can actually change and work with. In this sense limitation is the root of our expansion. In response to events we will transform ourselves. And this is the incredible thing about being human and possessing choice.

The Master And The Servant

This is how the Know Yourself method works. Your base Choleric temperament will always be consistently expressed and will colour the expression of the others as the base or master temperament makes use of the others employing the other traits almost like tools. They are referred to as the servants. However a secondary temperament will usually be the most active of the servants and your Choleric nature will utilise these tools more. If you are a complementary mix you will usually have a very consistent personality and if you are a non-complementary mix you will usually be unpredictable in your responses. This is not something to be conflicted about, it is something to embrace in order to master utilising your natural strengths.

I ignore the other temperaments expressed in you because you will naturally learn to master their expression as you continue to work on yourself.

Summary

You will find your pattern as a Choleric expressed in one of these three primal Choleric patterns. It is important to approach this with the attitude of discovery, so that you uncover what is hidden within you. There will be a temptation to attempt to make yourself fit into one of these rather than discovering your pattern. Though this is useful it will not unleash the simple power of the method. The entire creation is revelation and you are an integral part of it. The Know Yourself method opens up the revelation of your pattern to you in a manner that allows you to discover you and learn to make use of yourself by working with what is actually there. The modern maxim, 'You can be anything you want to be,' is revealed as a nonsense, for you are patterned and by granting yourself permission to be you, you open up the possibility of discovering not only your personality type's deep patterning but to accept those things that truly grant you fulfilment.

The Choleric-Melancholic

Introduction

The Choleric-Melancholic brings an incredible capacity to focus. This brings an active fiery, thoughtful nature, as if the fire drives through the earth. It is not a terribly balanced form but they are capable of driving forward intelligently with thought that is logical, with a Choleric who leaps to solutions that are intelligent and effective. Because this form combines Fire and Earth, we may think of stone arrowheads, they bring hard focus, penetration and an energy which drives forward. It combines two Elements which are similar by their dryness, which results in a complementary mixture. Fire and Earth mix well together and we may think of clay bricks and indeed this type builds projects well.

The problem here is inflexibility, a strong capacity to drive forward and a narrow health range, beyond which they become imbalanced. They have to work hard to overcome their tendency to burn-out and over-reach. With a balanced and appropriate approach they are simply incredible to watch in action. They will knowingly take immense risks, possessing the capacity to work out exactly what the risks are and how to mitigate them. When they burn out they become excessively and negatively melancholic. When beset by inflammatory patterns or psychological imbalance their fire rages uncontrollably and they become excessively melancholic and fearful.

Emotionally this is not a very stable form, so they will naturally protect themselves and their personal space, maintaining hard, sharp boundaries, with sharp tongues and a capacity to ruthlessly shed what they see as unnecessary or inappropriate relationships and activities.

The form is an easy one to master once they can see past the aura of strength that accompanies this type. What they must understand is that the range within which their strengths are effective is narrow and hence, they must pursue life balance and dietary common sense to remain within the narrow boundaries of their optimal health range.

This is a Choleric who deploys the rationale of a Melancholic to pursue Choleric strategies. They produce quick, thorough practical solutions, well thought out, efficient and courageous, without the typical Melancholic's procrastination. A sure sign of impending illness for this type is when melancholic procrastination starts to manifest. They should take procrastination as a warning sign of imbalance. However, where you find melancholic modalities in subjection to Choleric determinations then you are faced with a Melancholic-Choleric, combining procrastination with quick effective strategies, unlike the Choleric-Melancholic, who will rarely procrastinate so long as they are quite well.

The World According to the Choleric-Melancholic

CV

I get things done and I do not suffer fools gladly. You will know where you stand with me. I do not advise you to invade my personal domain without invitation, and don't expect a kind reception if you happen to make such a mistake. I may occasionally feel some remorse at the harshness of my reaction to you, but if you do it again you will most likely get a similar reaction. I need my boundaries respected.

I am definitely goal-oriented and although I love the aesthetic aspects I prefer practical workable solutions that allow me to respond readily. I think things through so don't tell me how to do things unless I ask you to, and when I do ask, please make your answers short and clear.

I have a strong sense of fairness and justice and am naturally a bit self-centred as I need to be protective of my narrow health range. Things are on my terms and my terms tend to win, so why would I change that. If you don't like it, then I suggest that you work with someone else more to your liking. I like to win and if you like winning too then you will have to adjust to my way of winning. If you want to challenge my methods then could you please think your arguments through and make them quickly and succinctly, as I really don't have all day. As I said earlier, I am fair and if what we are doing doesn't work I'll give you a fair hearing. If it does work, then all you need to do is to get on with the job in the way that works.

I have good, effective people skills, which are focussed on getting things done and not geared towards me pandering to anyone's ego. I will let you know my mind because it is better to be clear.

The Choleric-Melancholic Traits According to the World

You are active go getters with exceedingly strong minds, which make you natural leaders. You look after your team or group and will organise things in very straightforward ways. You get projects off the ground and organise running projects quickly, with ruthless efficiency and as much tact as gets the job done. Our feelings are definitely less important to you than the job at hand.

You are stimulating, interesting company and a loyal friend, though when people prove disloyal or stupid, you will, after having given them ample chance by your own measurement of justice, will sever all ties and send us packing far out of your sight. By this time even our remorse can't repair the damage done and so we will be dealt with summarily (and deservedly so from your perspective).

Relationships with you require the development of a thick skin for you must say and make clear what you see. This is often quite difficult to deal with and it tends to come very quickly and incisively.

Supporting you is difficult because of your strict boundaries; we have no choice but to broach them if we are to offer you support, and then you bristle and growl to protect the sanctity of your space and a sharp bite is just as likely. Romantic relationships are even harder!

As for getting you to change your mind? Well, that's a minefield! And you definitely have no fear of confrontation.

The Choleric-Melancholic Impulses

You want to get to action and so you close down options quickly as you drive towards the goal. You exist to bring projects into being and draw out of the creative source intellectually what will make that happen, with razor sharp focus. This brings a brash hot energy to the task. You solve problems quickly and non-methodically.

Excuses for those around you come from your sense of justice and so once they cross an invisible line the sword descends, swiftly and decisively, severing the metaphorical head, like a guillotine. Because of your sense of justice, idealism is a weakness to which you are prone, however once you are in a state of healthy balance you will appraise situations quickly and then act decisively.

Summary

The Choleric-Melancholic is a complementary mixture and so is a relatively easy form to master containing incredible possibilities. Essentially, we have a goal-oriented, hardworking, thinking type with creative and managerial potentialities. There is a need for intellectual stimulation and variety in projects, for they carry projects to completion swiftly.

This form is fair and just, but self-centred. To work with them we must be prepared for fireworks, and we must allow them to lead. Micromanaging this type is dangerous for your health.

The Choleric-Phlegmatic

Introduction

The Choleric-Phlegmatic is an active, empathetic, facilitative type. This is a Choleric with a strong intuitive and gently firm nature. The combination of the hot and cold natures as well as the dry and wet natures results in a very balanced and even natured type. This is perhaps the most balanced of the 'non-complementary' natures and it combines flexibility, drive, focus and a genius for observation. This is an even-tempered Choleric, outwardly active with an underlying sense of calm. The phlegmatic nature ensures that this goal-oriented Choleric doesn't waste time exploring avenues which they don't believe will achieve optimum results. Though this is a 'non-complementary' mixture, water heated by fire results in steam and this type can possess an almost sanguine capacity in company, with an ability to switch the engagement on or off at will. They are flexible and strong and usually compassionate.

To harness the power of this mixture they must stand apart to allow the clarity that the water offers to the fire. They need reflective time and space, which rekindles the fire. This type will slip around obstacles and sense challenges before they become apparent, with astonishing wisdom, timing and capacity for restraint.

This nurturing Choleric type will disengage and move on effortlessly to new projects and possibilities, and you may not even notice that they're gone.

The World According To The Choleric-Phlegmatic

CV

I love listening and observing people, from a position of deep stillness before committing to action. I move into action when it is clear how to act and what to do and I feel my way through the terrain, with a smooth unbroken energy. I very much rely upon feeling and intuition and so I often act in ways utterly contrary to the conventional wisdom but having paid close attention to what is happening now and has happened before, I am usually very certain of what I am doing. I don't hammer and drill my way in, but I flow through with a gentle determination that belies the presence of the force beneath.

I possess quiet strength and need quiet space. From that vantage point, I can detect and observe the deep currents that move people and trigger events; this is my genius. Think of me as a fiery fist in a soft velvet glove, that can strike you head-on, but prefers to deflect, parry, convince and resolve with wisdom, rather than main force.

I need space and can't understand why you make life so hard for yourselves! Leave me alone and let me engage with you when I am ready.

The Choleric-Phlegmatic Traits in the eyes of the World

We often notice your smooth, gentle energy, but you are impossible to engage with if you don't let us in. Conversation with you is interesting, stimulating and you bring such interesting insights and differing points of view, but then you're off without so much as a by your leave. You maintain your boundaries and a moat so broad that it is rarely clear where it begins, and because the drawbridge is always raised, people find themselves floundering across the moat, only to find in the end that you are nowhere to be seen anyway!

You succeed effortlessly, with incredible creativity and we have always benefited from your nurturing insightful nature.

The Choleric-Phlegmatic Impulses

You are suspended in an ocean of possibilities, relaxing and listening to the hidden songs within it, borne along passively on its deep currents wherever they choose to carry you. Then you move into action, bringing a supportive counterpoint to the isolated melody of the hidden song, so that its voice now rising, breaks the surface with soaring clarity. Throughout, your accompaniment will be that of midwife to the emerging theme. However, the more Choleric you are in nature, the more prone you become to imposing your own voicing upon the song. You insist, cajole and push towards exposure. You force things into the open and then, having released the music for all to hear, you want your freedom from a song whose melodies were familiar to you long before you raised them from depths previously silent to all but you. This makes you a natural pioneer and reveals a capacity for visionary, nurturing leadership.

Summary

The Choleric-Phlegmatic is a quietly active, intuitive type, who needs plenty of space and freedom to choose their projects. They are wonderful to have around if they wish to be with you. You have to work hard for their trust and companionship, for they keep themselves to themselves.

The Choleric Sanguine

Introduction

The Choleric-Sanguine is an active, busy, strongly communicative, restless and goal-oriented type. This is a driven, hot, creative and pioneering type. The hot, driving energy comes from the combination of the two hottest types, with the hottest of these two types being the basis of the bio-type. This 'complementary-mixture' brings the Sanguine's creativity, flexibility, changeability and curiosity, firmly under the governance of the Choleric's goal-oriented nature. They are consistently hot, active, creative and focused. The changeability brought by the Sanguine's nature is commandeered into making things happen and is consistently and regularly brought to bear. Fire drives wind hard to create a scirocco, a focussed tornado of hot changeable activity, burning through barriers and shattering constraints. Pinning this type down is impossible. To harness the power of this type you must ride its fire dragon and submit to its shifting, creative, penetrating, spinning energy.

Their generosity and loyalty are intense but conditional. Their energy seems boundless, and you wouldn't want them as an enemy.

The World According to the Choleric-Sanguine

CV

I am active, curious, courageous, fun and a great communicator. My goal-oriented, active, straightforward nature means that you will either love me or hate me, there are no in-betweens and to be honest I don't really care if you don't like me as long as you don't get in my way. I hold this as one of my greatest strengths as it gets things done and those who deliberately try to get in my way live to regret it. I am great both at getting projects off the ground and seeing them through. When starting projects my creative side brings my pioneering bent into play and when steering projects my communication and natural management skills come to the forefront. However, I do need to have people around me and given the choice, I prefer not to work alone. Choleric-phlegmatics can work alone, but I prefer teamwork.

I will regularly purge my impressive contact list of time-wasters. Although I'm talkative and friendly I'm more interested in the end goals than the texture of the journey, and so my social interactions will always tend to serve a clear purpose.

I will work my way through an array of possibilities as I explore the way forward and when called for, will change direction decisively and abruptly. Once I have narrowed the range of possibilities to the ones that I think will work I will quickly lock onto the target and focus in, but if something doesn't work, please do not be surprised if I reverse my opinion and reach for an option previously abandoned, and do not be surprised that when you point this out, I react by closing down the discussion with a guillotine. It will be fast, clever and cutting and may amount to pulling out of the hat an idea that you had suggested in the past that I had summarily discounted as being unworkable. If I offer you an apology or an acknowledgment, then know that you are dealing with a highly evolved Choleric-Sanguine and count your blessings.

I am not a people person for the sake of the company, I am a people person for the sake of my projects. I am thick skinned and am rarely offended but I will take stock of our exchanges, and they may well come back to haunt you.

I make things happen creatively and can communicate easily with creatives and management types. When the stage is mine, expect sharp anecdotes and metaphors which hit the mark with precision, and which allow me to drive my points home, often repeatedly, so that there can be no doubt that you've got it. I am also not averse to making U-turns or completely changing direction and dragging you off on a totally unexpected journey, just rest assured that in the end, and much faster than you may have expected, we will have arrived at the destination.

I am not arrogant. I am self-centred, self-assured and I make use of these traits to make things happen. If you think that I am arrogant (and I really don't care if you do) then I invite you to consider with care the fine distinctions that pertain between being self-centred, being self-assured and being arrogant.

The Choleric-Sanguine Traits in the Eyes of the World

You are interesting and difficult to be with, but sometimes fun. The intensity never ends and keeping up with you is exhausting. You possess personality by the truckload, and you suck up attention like an oxygen bomb. Your conversation is wide ranging, incisive and slices the issues apart in a way that gets quickly to the meat of the question. The conversation twists and turns, changing direction, writhing and turning through the issues, with leaps and jumps and insight upon insight.

We would describe you as generous, but to say easy-going would be a bit of a stretch. Enthusiasm and optimism are your natural gifts, and you smash open possibilities and transform situations or you reduce them to a scorched wasteland as you push forward and explore the possibilities (as to the wasteland, if you are on the receiving end, don't assume the existence of a well-developed conscience). We may find ourselves sorely disappointed. However, you promise the world and you deliver, and this trait is one that we are quite prepared to live with.

Our main complaint is that you will change direction and head off galloping towards the furthest horizon and we had better keep up because Heaven alone will have to help those who cannot stay the pace. We often experience this as heartless ruthlessness, but it becomes clear that you are more fixated upon the goals than the relationships. Confrontations with you are more like confronting the Roman army's scorched earth assaults. You raze the buildings and crops to the ground, conquer the inhabitants and execute the prisoners, so that they know that when you say, 'No one should leave by that door!' You are obeyed and you really won't care about the complaints.

You will not be contained and feel pressure to narrow your options, so you shut down alternatives and arguments swiftly and ruthlessly. There is very little time for malice, things just move much too quickly.

The Choleric-Sanguine Impulses

You stand just beyond the lip of the abyss, driving things forward. You will glance in to see what is coming quickly as you wind and whirl, weaving a manifestation in a Bagua Chang-like swimming movement of activity. You stride over the world and glance into the abyss, feeling its tremors and knowing how to bring forth its songs. Your hot nature causes you to marshal your gains efficiently. You know by doing and experience little regret over any 'collateral damage' that comes as an inevitable consequence of successful, decisive action. Your intuition is in action and when this source of certainty, which you hold within your hands begins to falter, then it is time to find a sheltered corner in which to realign.

Summary

This type must be actively engaged and able to actualise their impulses, which they get to know through action. They love to act and will communicate as a means to facilitate their aims. Organising, changing direction and making happen creatively is really what they were made to do.

Putting It All Together

Introduction

We have examined the Choleric and its three possible expressions. Their legendary single-mindedness and typical antics should be quite clear to you. This is just how they are wired. I hope that you've learnt lots, had fun and picked up some new insights. The point is to develop an intuitive grasp of the Choleric and learn how to deal with them and of course since this is a book written for Cholerics, you should have become a little clearer and more comfortable with yourself. You should now be ready to use this information to be a better Choleric, or just how best to deal with Cholerics (or rather be dealt with by Cholerics!). We are now at the third book and so bang in the middle of the series. And yes, I admit that it's taken me a long time to finish this series! Three guesses as to what my type is??? Please continue the journey with the coming books and just keep dipping into these treasure chests, they were designed to be looked into as a reminder and aid to reflection on our difficulties dealing with each other. Be brutally honest with yourself (Cholerics find it easier to be brutally honest with others!) but be gentle and merciful at the same time. The point is not to beat yourself up, it is to recognise your own antics, impulses and motivations, from a place that frees you to address them and to bring the natural best out of yourself. Time, success, failure, persistence and practice are your greatest friends on the journey. Let's re-examine the lessons we've learned, but remember that there is a lot more detail in the book.

The Lessons

The lessons are very simple:

1. Work with yourself not against yourself. You are you. You possess the fundamental qualities and impulses that you do. You would do well to get to know them like the back of your own hand. That is the point of 'Know Yourself'. Different situations will invariably surprise you as your potentialities reveal themselves.

2. Learn about your default reactions and what triggers them. Understand how that

happens, ignore the 'why' initially and really focus upon the 'how'. Learn when they are useful and when they are not. Then work at becoming more appropriate and this will bring wisdom.

3. By now you should realise that the other types have their natural strengths. Make life easy for yourself, copy them when you see that they have an instinctive genius for certain types of situations. Your arsenal of responses will increase.

4. Pay attention, reflect and change. Then pay attention, reflect and change. Then pay attention, reflect and change. Do it again, and then... Do it again. Ok, by now I think you get the point!

By paying attention we begin to grasp the nature of the interwoven tapestry of existence and we become better at understanding potentialities, possibilities and outcomes. Of course, we will get it wrong at times, but celebrate getting it wrong and really reflect on what happened and how you misread the situation. More often than not, we learn more from our errors than we do from getting it right.

Remember that people are what they are. They can change themselves and you can change yourself. Address that which you have the power to change, Yourself! Just be forgiving of the errors of others and watch that you don't fall prey to the faults which you have observed. That is hard work!

Benefit from the perspectives of the other types and practise empathising with those perspectives. You don't have to accept it, and it may be quite crazy to do so, but rather try to understand where those perspectives come from and how their experiences have contributed to their peculiar worldview. Invariably, this habit leads you to really examine your own perspectives. The differences that exist in the creation are a mercy!

In the words of Jalaluddin Rumi:

> "Yesterday I was clever, so I wanted to change the world. Today I am wise, so I am changing myself."

You are part of existence, therefore when you have changed, all of existence has changed.

Putting It into Practice

Pay attention, reflect and change! Let's wake up to the vast subtle tapestry of ourselves and the entire universe. Study how changing our behaviour transforms our perspectives. Study the jewel that is appropriateness and how that necessarily varies from creature to creature.

Releasing Our Stories on the Journey to Reality

Choleric! Your way isn't the only way.

Listen to the stories of others. You have much to learn from your opposite biotype, the Phlegmatic. And if you have married a Phlegmatic, then forgive me for giggling!

Enjoying & Employing Natural Strengths

Enjoy your natural strengths and employ them. Observe the natural strengths of others and study how to benefit by them. Of course, that sounds pretty simple in principle but by now, we all know how difficult that will be to put into practice.

The Next Step

If you want to learn more about the other types read:

- **Know Yourself Sanguine** - This explores the Sanguine and the different sanguine combinations

- **Know Yourself Melancholic** - This explores the Melancholic and the different melancholic combinations

- **Know Yourself Phlegmatic** - This explores the Phlegmatic and the different phlegmatic combinations

Ok, now I'm off to start writing Know Yourself Melancholic. Oh, that should be fun!

www.ingramcontent.com/pod-product-compliance
Lightning Source LLC
Chambersburg PA
CBHW050128280326
41933CB00010B/1292